MY AMERICA

For my Havana and Mathilda

MY AMERICA

CHRISTOPHER MORRIS

STEIDL

For 15 years I have been photographing wars around the world. After the birth
of my daughters I knew that I wanted a change. In the year 2000 I turned away
from wars and set out traveling across the United States documenting President
George W. Bush for TIME magazine.

What I discovered was a people in love with their country and their President,
a culture of American society that had found a "divine" Bush. *MY AMERICA*
is a chronicle of this journey.

–Christopher Morris 2005

E PLURIBUS UNUM
"OUT OF MANY ONE"

Washington, D.C. 2004

Wells, Maine 2004

Harrisburg, Pennsylvania 2004

Vienna, Ohio 2004

Washington, D.C. 2004

Philadelphia, Pennsylvania 2004

Lexington, Kentucky 2003

Liberty, Missouri 2004

Twentynine Palms, California 2004

Tampa, Florida 2004

Lancaster County, Pennsylvania 2004

Steidl
Vale Studio
62 Wood Vale
London SE23 3ED
United Kingdom

Dear Book Collector

Thank you for buying one of our books.

We create the finest books on photography, contemporary art, fashion and literature. Steidl books are renowned worldwide for their incisive content and unparalleled production values. If you would like to receive our free catalogue, or for us to keep you up to date about our books, special offers and events, please fill out and return this card or visit our website at www.steidlville.com

Join our book club at www.steidlville.com/bookclub and receive benefits such as members only discounts, signed copies and priority booking for special events.

First Name _____ Last Name _____

Address _____

City _____ Post/Zip Code _____

Country _____ Email _____

Please send me:
- ☐ a free catalogue ☐ email newsletters
- ☐ details of special promotions and events by post

STEIDL

Welcome to Steidlville.com

Saginaw, Michigan 2004

Dinuba, California 2003

Tampa, Florida 2004

Tampa, Florida 2004

Greensboro, Georgia 2003

HPB-5

Fridley, Minnesota 2003

Washington, D.C. 2005

Honolulu, Hawaii 2003

Dallas, Texas 2006

Manchester, New Hampshire 2004

Washington, D.C. 2005

Portsmouth, New Hampshire 2003

Washington, D.C. 2004

Louisville, Kentucky 2004

Nampa, Idaho 2005

Hudson, Wisconsin 2004

Guantanamo Bay, Cuba 2003

Crawford, Texas 2005

Dinuba, California 2003

Westlake, Ohio, 2004

Columbus, Ohio 2004

Fridley, Minnesota 2003

Pearl Harbor, Hawaii 2003

Pensacola, Florida 2004

Washington, D.C. 2005

Washington, D.C. 2005

Fayetteville, North Carolina 2005

Dallas, Texas 2004

Dallas, Texas 2004

Philadelphia, Pennsylvania 2004

Westlake, Ohio 2004

Westlake, Ohio 2004

Philadelphia, Pennsylvania 2004

Camp Pendleton, California 2004

Greeley, Colorado 2004

Chalmette, Louisiana 2005

Istanbul, Turkey 2004

Istanbul, Turkey 2004

Saginaw, Michigan 2004

Washington, D.C. 2005

Washington, D.C. 2005

Washington, D.C. 2005

Farmington Hills, Michigan 2004

Annandale, Virginia 2004

Saginaw, Michigan 2004

New York, New York 2004

Washington, D.C. 2003

Washington, D.C. 2005

Westlake, Ohio 2004

Phoenix, Arizona 2004

Pontiac, Michigan 2004

Washington, D.C. 2003

Coronado, California 2005

Tampa, Florida 2004

Pontiac, Michigan 2004

Ft. Lewis, Washington 2004

El Dorado, Arkansas 2004

Honolulu, Hawaii 2003

Louisville, Kentucky 2004

Cincinnati, Ohio 2004

Columbus, Ohio 2005

Fayetteville, North Carolina 2005

Fayetteville, North Carolina 2005

Fayetteville, North Carolina 2005

Fridley, Minnesota 2003

Washington, D.C. 2005

Omaha, Nebraska 2005

Crawford, Texas 2005

Stratham, New Hampshire 2004

Washington, D.C. 2005

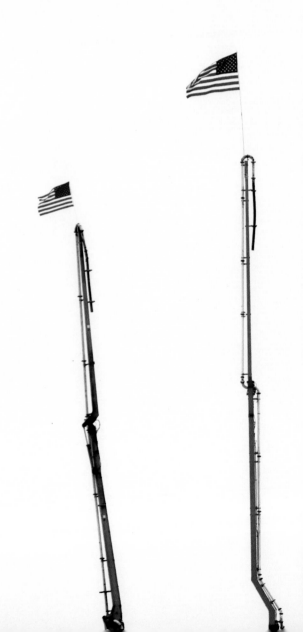

Springfield, Missouri 2004

Manchester, New Hampshire 2004

Washington, D.C. 2003

Guantanamo Bay, Cuba 2003

Traverse City, Michigan 2004

Hudson, Wisconsin 2004

Fargo, North Dakota 2005

Killeen, Texas 2005

Cuyahoga Falls, Ohio 2004

Sea Island, Georgia 2004

Washington, D.C. 2005

New York, New York 2004

Acknowledgments

All of this work was produced while on assignment for Time magazine.
Without the support of my editors, Michele Stephenson, MaryAnne Golon, Alice Gabriner,
Hillary Raskin and the entire photo staff at Time magazine, none of this photography would have
been possible. With special thanks to Alice, who early on in my project gave me guidance and
encouragement to continue.

Thanks to Howard Chapnick, Claudia Christen, Enrico Dagnino, Luc Delahaye, Frank Evers,
Mary Goldman, Sarah Hasted, Bill Hunt, Margaret Lafaro, Yukiko Launois, Jean-Francois Leroy,
Dave Metz, Grazia Neri, Robert Peacock, Gilles Peress, Charles Ommanney, Kathy Ryan,
Gerhard Steidl, Robert Stevens, Kenneth Troiano, Garrett White, all my colleagues at VII,
my mother and father, and my lovely wife Vesna.

Thank you.

First edition 2006

Photo editing by Christopher Morris and Claudia Christen
Book and jacket design by Claudia Christen
Produced by Garrett White, New York

Copyright © 2006 Christopher Morris for the photographs and text
Copyright © 2006 Steidl Publishers for this edition

Production and printing by Steidl, Göttingen, Germany

Steidl
Düstere Strasse 4
D-37073 Göttingen
Germany

Phone + 49 551 49 60 60
Fax + 49 551 49 60 649
Email mail@steidl.de
www.steidl.de
www.steidlville.com

ISBN 3-86521-201-8
ISBN 13: 978-3-86521-201-6

Printed in Germany